The Camel Carrying Words In His Hump

Bahareh Amidi

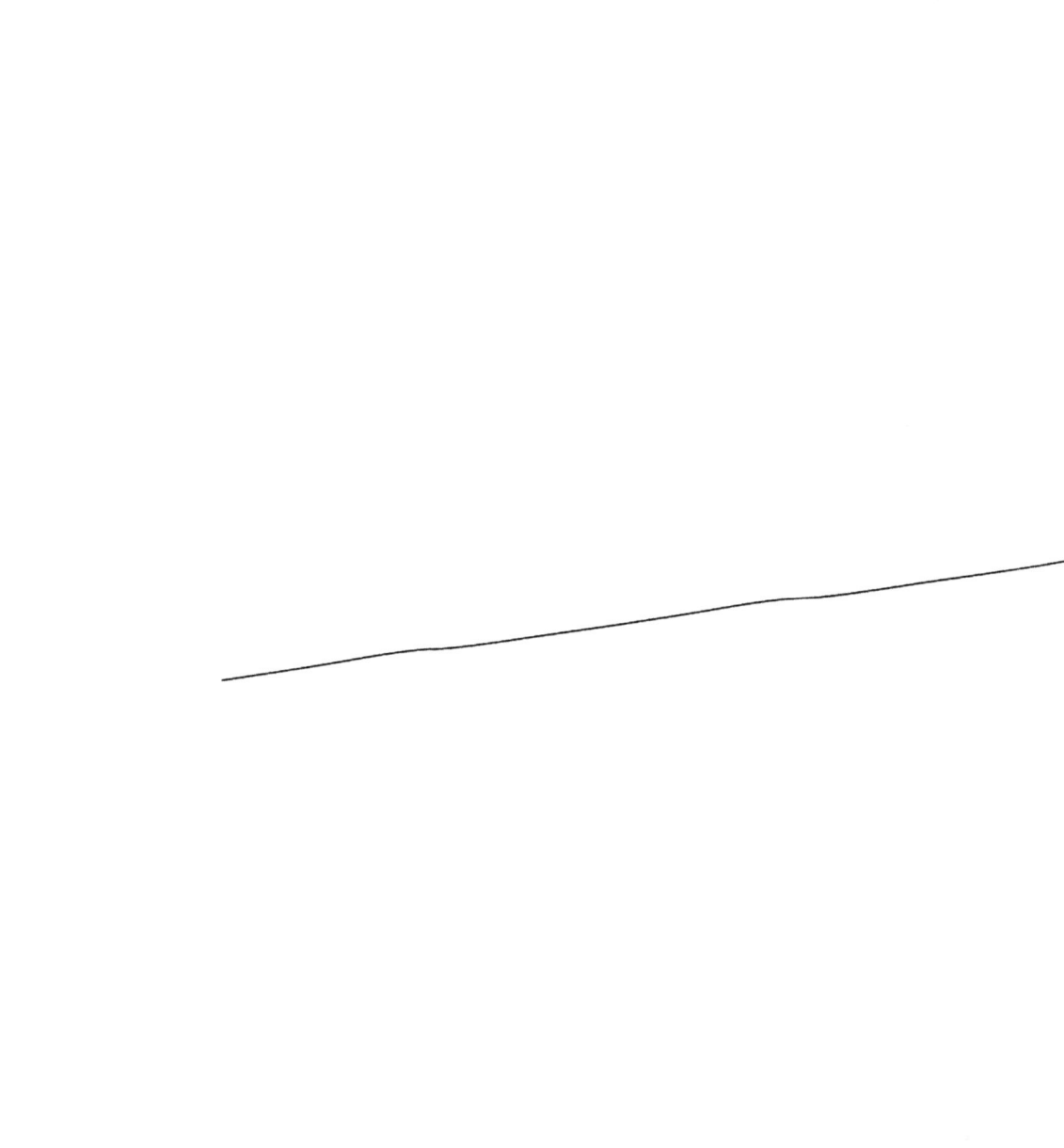

The Camel Carrying Words In His Hump

ISBN 979-8-9926240-1-4

cover and interior illustrations by
  Adora:
   @AdoraArts

email: connect@bahareh.com
facebook.com/Bahareh.Amidi
twitter.com/BaharehAmidi
youtube.com/baharehLIVE
instagram.com/bahareh_poetess
www.bahareh.com

"It is the last straw that breaks the camel's back."

—Charles Dickens

Listen to The Camel Carrying Words In His Hump

Once upon a time
there was a camel
This camel like many others
traveled patiently in the desert
This camel unlike all the rest
carried no water in his hump
He carried only words

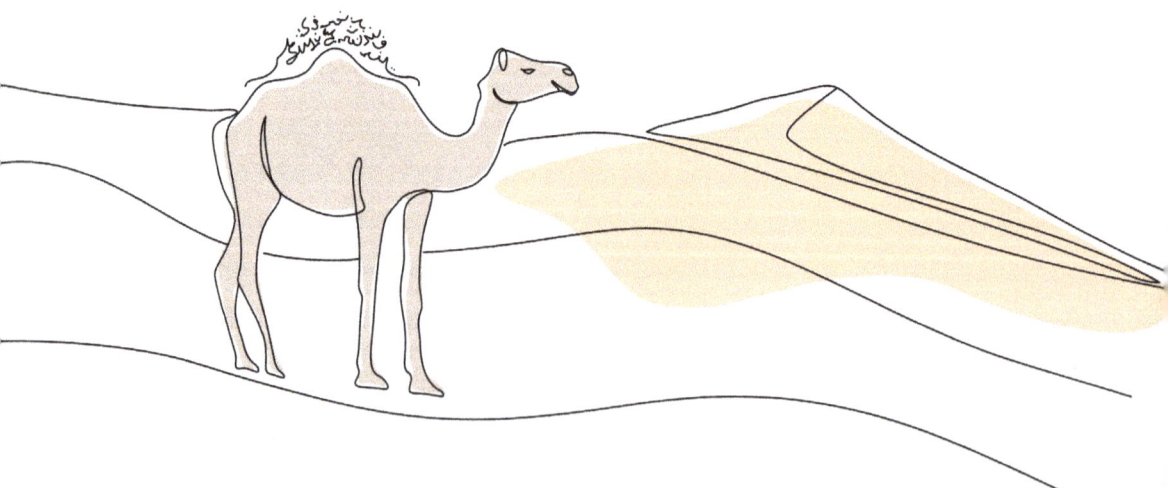

Throughout the centuries
as his ancestors had walked on the hot sands
and heard the tale of the traveling Nomads
the words had been collecting
until the day
the Patient one was born
with all the words on his back

Carrying the words
of brides and grooms
and also of the members of the clan
carrying their dead to the grave
Carrying truths and lies
The same words carrying healing light
and stabbing swords

The words of the ancient medicine men
and the words of the mama
helping mothers give birth
The words of the warriors of life
and also warriors killing to remain alive

The camel carried sounds of cries
and the whispers of tomorrows
that had not yet arrived
The camel carried
the laughter of the young
and the despair
of the old ones forgotten

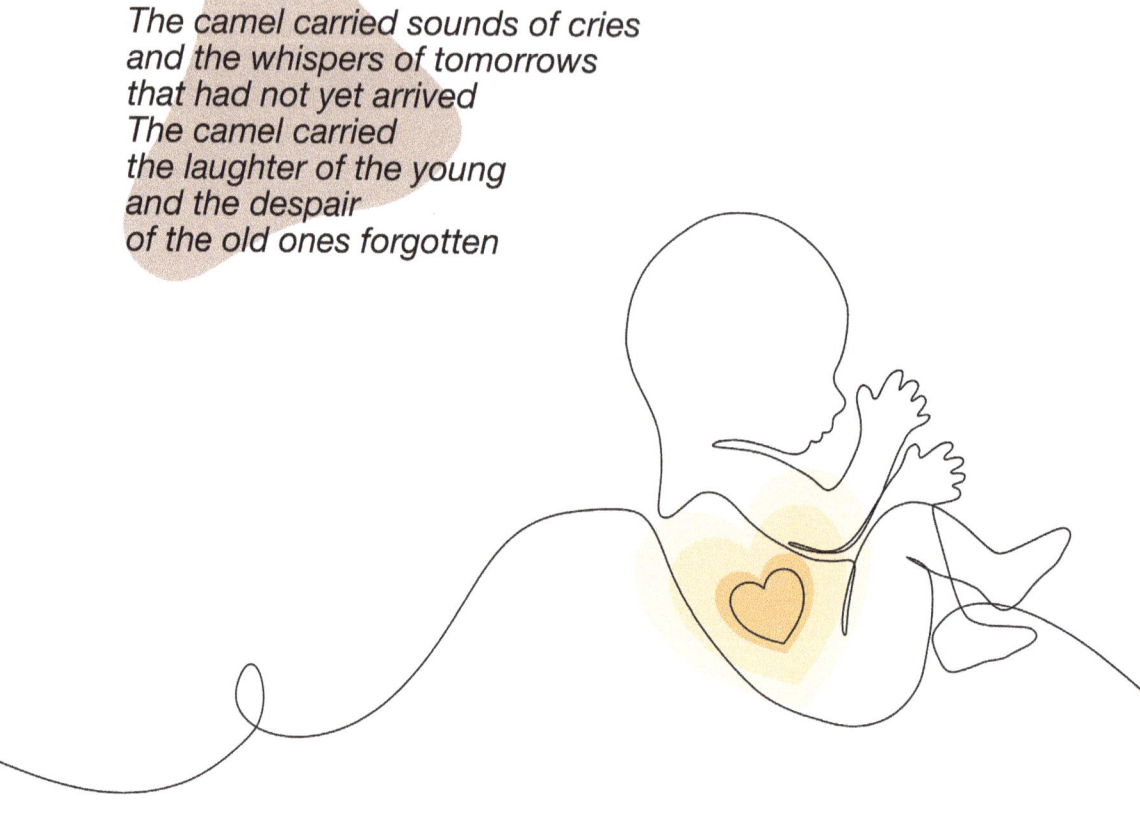

The words carried carefully
and tenderly and presently in the hump
Like seeds in gestation
waiting to be watered given life through light
Even those words
never spoken but only thought
All

All the words
    that have broken hearts
        and mended wounds
All the words
    that have started wars
        and ended lives
All the words
    full of life
        and no life at all

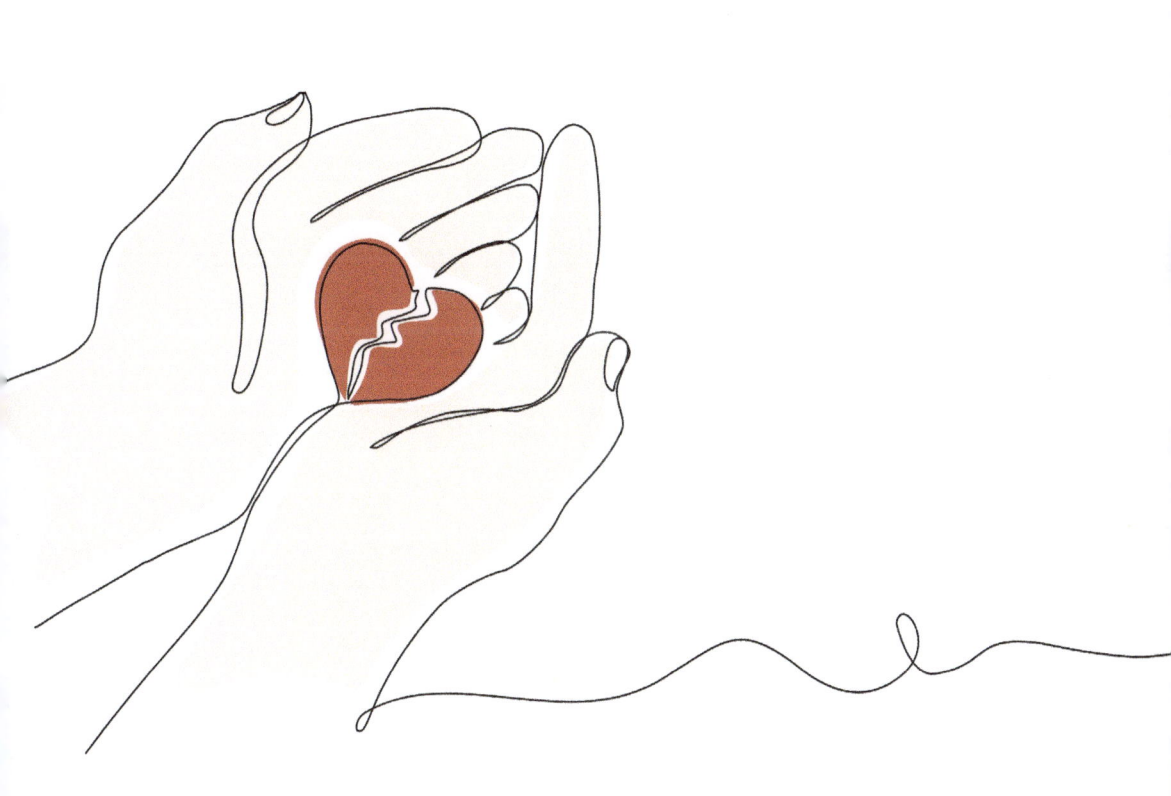

The beautiful image of the camel
walking through life
with all the words in his hump
The reflection
can be seen only in oasis
and in a moonlit sky

The words can only be seen
by the ready and pure in heart

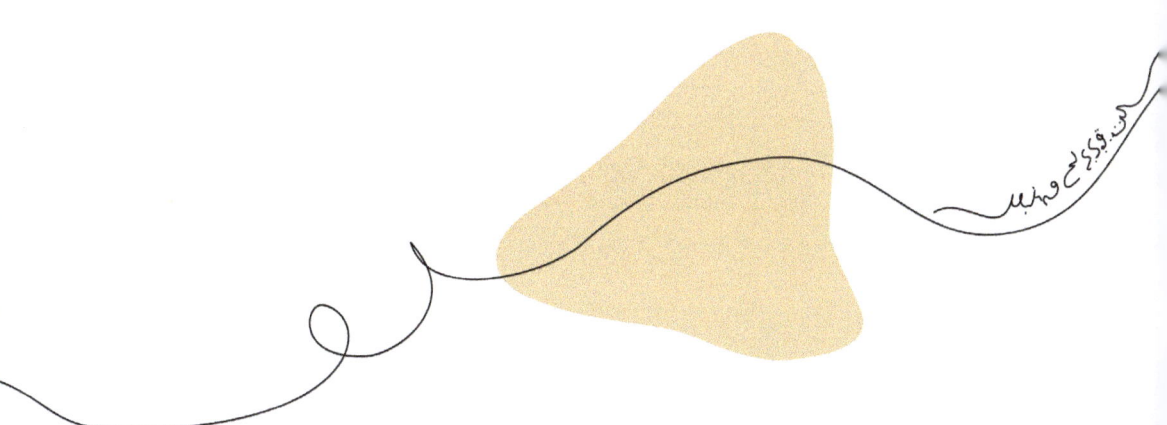

The language is universal
Every wise man and scholar
can understand
but also each child
not bearing a word on his tongue can feel

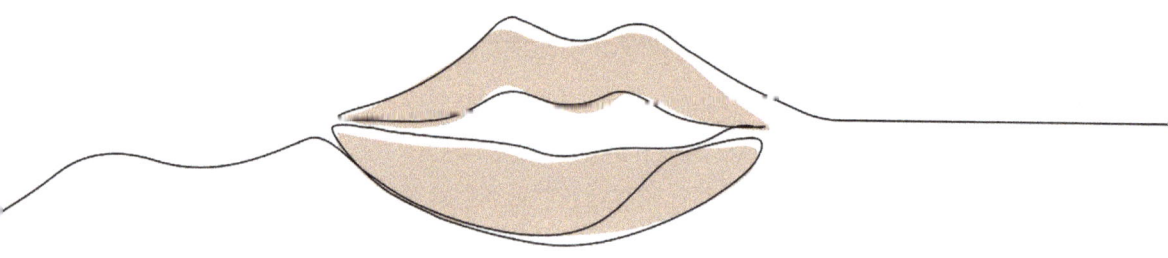

The blind man can add words
to the back of his knowledge
with his vision
The crippled man can add steps
to the ladder leading to heaven
with his words paving the way

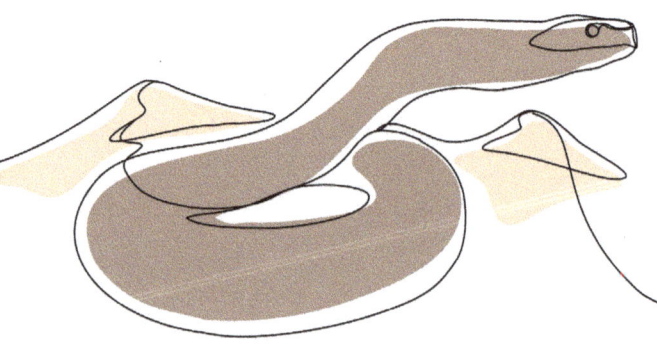

The deaf can hear the slithering of the snake
on the sand
and without word draw the poison out
and release light

The dumb man can speak
for a hundred and one nights
stringing together the words
from the one humped camel
The beauty of such wisdom
being carried in one hump

The same camel has carried
thousands and journals empty of words
and also thousands of books
with meaningless sentences upon sentences
trying to bring forth points of views
From all that the camel has observed only

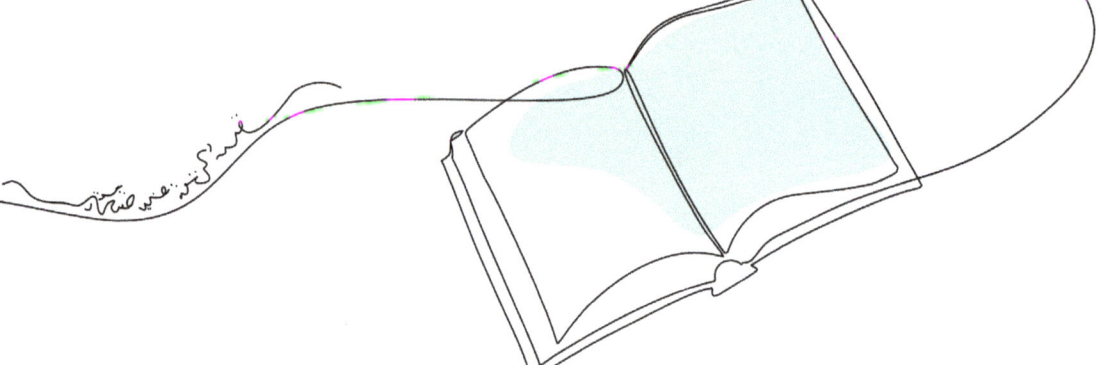

The observations of the eye
The absorptions of the skin
The taste of the mist
in the heat of the day
The sense of the touch
of the sand on the hoofs
All carried

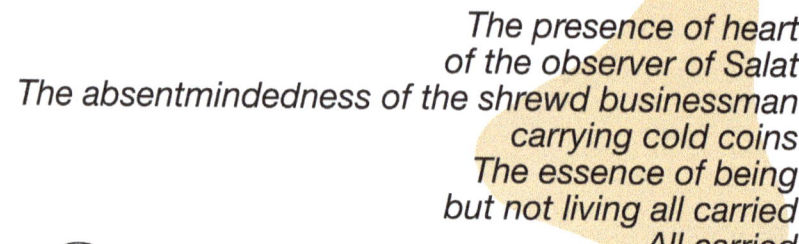

The presence of heart
of the observer of Salat
The absentmindedness of the shrewd businessman
carrying cold coins
The essence of being
but not living all carried
All carried

All contained
All present
All omnipresent
The camel
that carried the weight of all
but left no footprints
in the sand
All
Here
Now

All the words
All the wisdom
All the sorrows
All the joys
All carried HERE
Now
Ready to Deliver

www.ingramcontent.com/pod-product-compliance
Lightning Source LLC
Chambersburg PA
CBHW041544120626
46551CB00019B/2827